THE W
ACCORDING TO KIDS

Sally Collings

THE WORLD ACCORDING TO KIDS

A child's eye view of life,
love and chocolate cake

Sally Collings

HarperCollins*Publishers*

HarperCollins*Publishers*

First published in Australia in 2009
by HarperCollins*Publishers* Australia Pty Limited
ABN 36 009 913 517
www.harpercollins.com.au

HarperCollins*Publishers*

25 Ryde Road, Pymble, Sydney, NSW 2073, Australia
31 View Road, Glenfield, Auckland 0627, New Zealand
A 53, Sector 57, Noida, UP, India
77–85 Fulham Palace Road, London, W6 8JB, United Kingdom
2 Bloor Street East, 20th floor, Toronto, Ontario M4W 1A8, Canada
10 East 53rd Street, New York NY 10022, USA

National Library of Australia Cataloguing-in-Publication data:
Author: Collings, Sally.
Title: The world according to kids / Sally Collings.
ISBN: 9780732289768 (pbk.)
Subjects: Children--Quotation, Children--Humor.
Dewey Number: 828.02

Cover and internal illustrations by Emma Magenta
Cover and internal design by Jay Ryves, Future Classic
Typeset in Proforma by Jay Ryves & Hazel Lam, Future Classic
Printed and bound in Australia by Griffin Press on 100gsm offset

5 4 3 2 1   09 10 11 12

For Bethany and Sophia,
who are wise and funny in equal
measure every single day.

The web is a large and mysterious place ... some of these quotes have been passed on from blog to email to Facebook to dinner party. Despite my best detective work, I couldn't always find where they came from, but I've included a sprinkling of anonymous-source contributions here because they are just so funny. Apologies to anyone whom I didn't contact directly to ask for their permission; please get in touch with the publishers so we can include a note in future editions.

Introduction

It all began when I started asking people, 'What's the funniest thing your child has ever said?' Most people had an answer (or a hundred); some even had journals and scrapbooks to show me, lovingly recording their children's endearing, crazy and sometimes downright indecent sayings.

Then the children had their turn. I asked them to share their world view by answering questions like 'How do you make friends?', 'What is the sun made of?' and 'Where do we go when we die?' Some took home questionnaires from their schools, while others joined in discussion groups at their kindergartens. The results are not only hilarious and off-the-wall, but unnervingly close to the bone, and at times so true it takes your breath away.

Children are like little aliens among us (cute little *Toy Story*-style aliens, of course, rather than the scary people-eating variety). Their job here is to learn how this strange new world works. To kids, most things adults do are pretty weird. It's all new to them, after all. They are not born knowing the rules. Such as that you shouldn't try to baptise a cat, or that women's upper arms get wobbly with age (Why, Lord? Why?), or that mums are always right. But they learn.

And we learn along with them. As their parents, teachers, companions and carers, we discover that no matter how hard we try to hide it, kids know if we're angry (especially if we're brushing their hair at the time). We find out that chocolate is kind of good for us because it's got milk in it. And that love is what's in the room at Christmas if we stop opening presents and listen.

Welcome to the world according to kids.

When I was a baby...

When I was a baby I looked like a bear. My dad said that I walked like a bear because I loved honey and peanut butter.
Harry, 4

I looked like a falcon – I had a blue beak and black feathers.
Rory, 4

I was like a crocodile – like a big one.
Oscar, 4

When I was a baby I was very relational and cute.
I had big blue eyes and was petrified of flies.
Shona, 12

I was like a bottle.
Freddie, 3

When I was little ...

I wriggled around a lot. I was small, about the size of some shelves.
Michael, 4

I must have been cow-like because since I was born I've
had the name Milly-molly-moo-cow.
Sophia, 10

I was small, cute and bald.
Mackenzie, 10

I was kind, quiet, and creative.
Eilis, 11

Life essentials

Dummy, milk, blue bear please NOW!
Jayden, 2

The best thing about brothers and sisters...

The best thing is that you have someone to talk to. Some are a lot older than me and they're fun and they're easy to annoy.
Sophia, 10

The worst thing about brothers and sisters...

The worst thing is they're all older so they think they're the boss.
Sophia, 10

You can't marry them.
Aidan, 5

Play nicely, kids

I'll get ya and it'll look like a bloody accident.
Edward, 7

That girl says she's gunna kick me in the nuts!
New acquaintance of Charli G, 4 (who was in hot pursuit)

I know at kinder I have to keep my hands to myself,
but don't think I'm going to do it here, because I'm not.
Benjamin, 3

(While putting the bike pump into her sister's ear)
I'm just going to blow her up.
Zoe, 5

(After giving his two-year-old sister a crew cut)
She wanted me to cut her hair.
Edward, 4

9

A sweet thought

Don't ever be too full for dessert.
Kelly, 10

Custard is important. It's not crunchy, it's soft. It makes you good.
Archie, 6

Hayden, 3 (who has a peanut allergy): Doughnuts make me sick.
Mum: No sweetheart, peanuts make you sick.
Hayden: Oh, well, doughnuts make me better?

Chocolate! It's yummy and it's got a little bit of milk,
which is kind of good for you.
Holly I, 8

Forget the cake, go for the icing.
Cynthia, 8

I just don't like it

Mummy, I can't eat my lunch. It might make me sick.
Alexander, 3

I hate bananas because I hate the taste, I hate the smell
and I hate everything about them. I don't like sitting
next to people eating bananas.
Gracie, 7

Stay away from prunes.
Randy, 9

I don't like salmon mornay. It tastes too fishy.
Meara, 8

Chocolate – it's not good for you and I just don't like it.
Aidan, 5

On vegetables

Mummy, I can't eat them because my taste bugs haven't grown up yet.
Olivia, 5

Brussels sprouts have peas in them and I hate peas.
Lincs, 5

You can't hide a piece of broccoli in a glass of milk.
Armir, 9

Where does the food go?

It goes down our neck, into our food sack and mixes up with liquid that grinds it up. It comes out as poop.
Gracie, 7

It goes down a little food drain that's squishy, it crunches up into pieces and comes out our bum.
Niamh, 5

It digests, goes into our tummy and comes out, you know, the rude bit.
Holly, 8

It gets sorted into good and bad piles in your tummy.
Stafford, 8

It comes into our brain.
Ned, 4

I eat noodles, then they go into my tummy, then into my knees, then that's it, nowhere else.
Fred, 3

Toilet time

I wanna poo in the bath.
Brayden, 2

(While running to the toilet)
Stay in there wee-wee, I'm putting you in the toilet.
Georgia, 3

(Pointing to his bottom)
I got a frog in there.
Alexander, 2

Oh mum, that was just awful. Getting poo on my finger
was worser than DYING.
Jade, 4

Best behaviour

I did a little bit of naughty things today, mummy. It was an accident,
I didn't mean to do it. I not do that any more.
Georgia, 3

(On being told 'You've been such a good girl this morning')
You mean when I was sleeping?
Josie, 4

Why do I have to go to school?

Because if you didn't go to school you wouldn't be able to learn anything and you would grow up to be quite stupid.
Mia, 7

Because children need to have a run and school has a bigger yard.
Eve, 5

To be educated to be smarter and plus, it's the law.
Mackenzie B, 10

You don't have to but it's best to. At school you learn stuff so you can go to work and make money. Also so the teachers get employed.
Charlotte W, 11

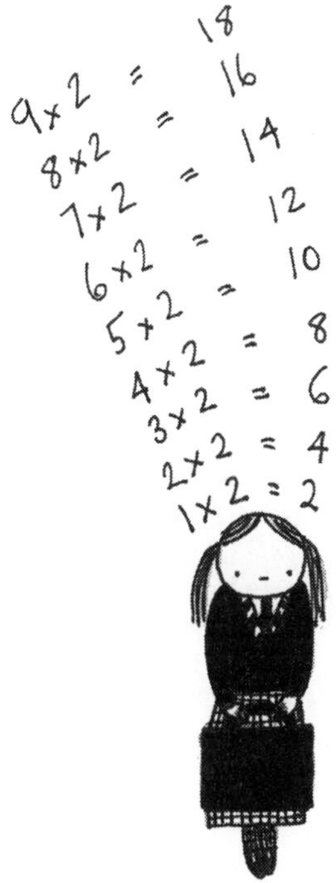
9x2 = 18
8x2 = 16
7x2 = 14
6x2 = 12
5x2 = 10
4x2 = 8
3x2 = 6
2x2 = 4
1x2 = 2

Making friends

Just be yourself and they will come.
Greta, 10

I know that someone is my friend when they play with you and laugh with you, not at you, and when you get a feeling you can trust them.
Charlotte, 11

I know that someone is my friend when I make a fool of myself and they act like I never did.
Shona G, 12

Here's the best way to make friends: 1. Say 'Hello'. 2. Say 'Do you want to play with me?' 3. Keep doing that.
Meara, 8

Advice for the new kid at school

Listen to everything the teacher says and don't look forward
to the next twelve years.
Isabelle, 12

Never talk back to a teacher whose eyes and ears are twitching.
Andrew, 9

Don't jump into a group too quickly. Wait and observe their true
personalities so you can see which ones you like best.
Shona, 12

Be happy, don't worry about it, you'll get some lunch breaks.
Holly Isabel, 8

The school pecking order

There's the downcast, the middlecast and the uppercast.
The downcast play baby games and can also be the not-nice girls;
the uppercast are the ones who everyone wants to be friends with.
I'm between the middle and the upper.
Stella V, 10

28

Imagine that

(Waking suddenly after her first memory of a dream)
Mummy! I've got movies behind my eyes!
Greta, 3

When you close your eyes and open them quickly, you can see rainbows.
Jack, 4

(Playing with Thomas the Tank Engine train on flour emptied
all over the pantry shelf)
Look, Mum, Thomas is playing in the snow!
Jasper, 2

(Balancing on two ice-cube trays on the kitchen floor)
I'm pretending to be on a skateboard.
Jasper, 20 months

I am Captain Snailbrain of the Smelly Disgusting Insect Spy Agency!
Finn, 6

Tell me a story – a very, very, very, very big story – about a melty biscuit.
Stella R, 4

The truth about television

People die but TV just goes on and on forever.
Rosa, 4

Mum: Oliver, you shouldn't be watching that program, it's scary.
Oliver, 3: It's okay, mum, they're just using their imagination.

Word power

I will call them dinosaur birds, cause I can't say pterodactyls.
Jack, 2

I need to get my fluid as I am dehyflated.
Georgia, 5

I like polluting my juice with water.
Stella V, 9

(Refusing an injection)
No injury!
Georgia, 3

I didn't do it on purple, Mummy.
Edward, 4

Sticks and stones may break my bones but your words
are hurting my ears.
Ethan, 4

Mummy, I'm very sosisticated.
Stella R, 9

(As his block tower fell over)
Oh, for chuck steak!
Jasper, 2

grrrrrl

Kidictionary

The book we look for erections in = street directory
Cleo, 3

Window screamers = windscreen wipers
Alex, 4

Hyena shoes = high heels
Georgia, 3

Wrist clock = watch
Jack, 4

De-good-en-ised = something spoilt
Jacquelyn, 8

Moon ice = hail
Bethany, 4

Spacelight = torch
Jack H, 4

'Up and down' planes = quick flights, no DVDs or food provided
Jack, 4

Getting away from it all

I run away, I go on holidays.
Jayden, 2

My perfect holiday would be going skiing like dad promised since I was
in year two. Every year he said we would but no! Now I'm in year six!
Charlotte W, 11

My perfect holiday would be on a beach with soft white sand and clean
blue water with palm trees and servants.
Eilis, 11

We have holidays because we don't get to see our mum and dad
at school.
Clancy, 6

Birthday treats

For my birthday I'm going to have a surprise party.
Rosa, 4

I'm the boss on my birthday and I get presents.
Greta, 10

My favourite thing to do at birthday parties is opening presents,
because I want to know what the present is.
Clancy, 6

(On his seventh birthday, which was also a school day)
This is just an ordinary day but with cupcakes.
Jack, 7

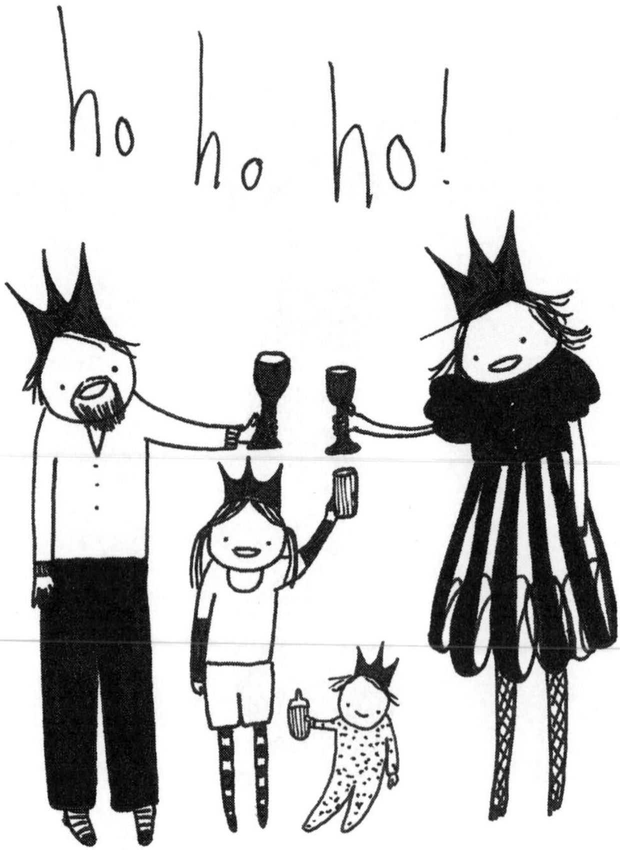
ho ho ho!

Merry Christmas

(On being told there were still two more sleeps until Santa came)
Is Santa getting off his chair?
Georgia, 2

I love it when all the family gets together and sits around the table
eating food and telling really, really bad jokes from Christmas crackers.
Sophia, 10

Christmas is celebrating life.
Meara, 8

Christmas is all about families, brandy and love.
Stella V, 7

Complete pet care

If I had a horse I would give it fresh water every morning, feed it, give it plenty of sunshine and baths, make sure it's happy every day. If it's not very interested in water or anything else, I would just go and sit down and read a book with it.
Kimmi, 5

(Because of cat flu, Jasper's cat had runny eyes)
Poor Smudge, you're crying. You need to have a dummy, that'll make you feel better.
Jasper, 2

(On the arrival of her new dog)
Okay darling, I'm your mummy.
Stella V, 6

Never try to baptise a cat.
Eileen, 8

Never hold a dust buster and a cat at the same time.
Kyoyo, 9

I sit on the cat, daddy?
Jayden, 2

Rules to live by

If you want a kitten, start out by asking for a horse.
Naomi, 15

Never spit when on a roller coaster.
Scott, 11

Don't squat with your spurs on.
Noronha, 13

Never trust a dog to watch your food.
Patrick, 10

Listen to your brain. It has lots of information.
Chelsey, 7

When your mum is mad at your dad, don't let her brush your hair.
Taylia, 11

Never tell your mum her diet's not working.
Michael, 14

Never bug a pregnant mum.
Nicholas, 11

How the world works

(When asked if he would like to go to the London Olympics)
I'll go in the running, but I'm not doing the gymnastics.
Harry P, 3

(Explaining what rugby players do)
They stand up and trip.
Alex, 4

Hairdresser: Please look down at your toes, hon.
Oliver, 3 (apologetically): I can't, my shoes are in the way.

Dad: On the farm, the farmer has a big animal with horns and a ring through his nose, called a ...
Oliver: Bull!
Dad: And when the bull gets married, who does he marry?
Oliver: A cow.
Dad: And when the bull and the cow have babies, what do they have?
Oliver: A fight!

Clothes and grooming

(On seeing a very glamorous birthday party dress)
Stella V, 7: I must buy that for my next party.
Mum: It's too expensive.
Stella: That's okay, I have £3 million in my bank account.

I need to put shorts on for playing with the boys because boys are very runny.
Alexa, 6

Felt markers are not good to use as lipstick.
Lauren, 9

Sleep in your clothes so you'll be dressed in the morning.
Stephanie, 8

Don't wear polka-dot underwear under white shorts.
Kellie, 11

I know my older sister loves me because she gives me all her old clothes and has to go out and buy new ones.
Lauren, 4

I have nothing to wear!
Charli G, 3

X

Cars

(Seeing the rain on her family's brand new car)
Oh no, this one is wet – we need a new one.
Peggy, 2

(Seeing her uncle's Jeep without the hardtop on)
Uncle Mia, someone cut your car.
Juliana, 3

Never dare your little brother to paint the family car.
Phillip, 13

roar

Emergency procedures

(Watching mum painting)
Mum: Harry, if I fell from the ladder would you ring the ambulance so they could come and help me?
Harry P, 4: Yes, mum.
Mum: How would you ring them?
Harry: I would dial ooo and press the green button.
Mum: Great. So just tell me again what you would do.
Harry: I would dial ooo, press the green button, then the ambulance would come ... and they would do the painting for you.

(While holidaying in Japan)
Stella R, 8: If there is an earthquake here and you and Daddy die, who will look after me?
Mum: Uncle Jimmy.
Stella: How will he know?
Mum: From our papers.
Stella: How will I get there?
Mum: He'll come to fetch you.
Stella: Who will get your money?

Save yourself – there's a lion. Run. Run.
Austin, 2

The big questions

When will I be grown up?

When I die, will I still be able to talk?

Are there other worlds in the sky?

How do you build this world?

When is the end of the world?

What does the end of the world look like?

Does the sun have birthdays?

Jack, 4

More big questions

Who decides what the weather will be like today?
Anna, 4

Mum, do you know how to realise?
Lanaya, 4

Alex, 5: How do you grow a moustache?
Dad: You let the hair on your face grow.
Alex: Do you water it?

Mum, did you know ants are an endangered species? They are in danger of being trodden on.
Stephanie, 3

After the farmer has taken the meat from the sheep, does he stitch it back up so it will be okay?
Alexa, 6

How do teeth help your mouth talk? Are they magic?
Alexander, 5

Can't they turn the fireworks to mute?
Stella V, 10

The painful truth

Mummy, why are your muscles underneath your arm and everyone else's are on top?
Callum, 7

(On seeing a mum's 'tuckshop arms')
What's that hanging under there? Urgh! What is it?
Nigel, 7

Dad, why do you always wear such big pants? Mummy always wears little pants.
Alex, 4

(Seeing mum's stomach two days after giving birth to baby number three)
Is another baby going to come out, mummy?
Edward, 4

Boys' toys

I don't have to put the toilet seat up when I wee, cos I got a big penis.
Jacob, 3

(When unable to wee before a long car trip)
My willy's tired.
Aussy, 3

Boys have a pagina and girls have a peanut.
Charli, 3

Why do girls only have bottoms?
Alex, 5

(In the shower with daddy)
Austin, 4: Daddy, my willy's small.
Daddy: What makes you say that?
Austin: My voice.

How the body works: babies

If you find a boy you want to marry you get a baby in your tummy.
Eve, 5

Babies grow in the tummy. You chop the tummy.
Charlie S, 5

Babies get born through a hole made by a knife.
Tara, 7

How the body works: blood

The chest pumper makes the blood go round our bodies.
Sienna, 6

The little purple pipes on the back of our arms, they let the
blood run through your body.
Michael, 4

The middle wife

This story was told by an anonymous second-grade teacher.

One day Erica takes her turn at show-and-tell, and waddles up to the front of the class with a pillow stuffed under her jumper. She holds up a snapshot of a baby. 'This is Luke, my baby brother, and I'm going to tell you about his birthday.

'First, mum and dad made him as a symbol of their love, and then dad put a seed in my mum's stomach, and Luke grew in there. He ate for nine months through an umbrella cord.

'Then, about two Saturdays ago, my mum starts going, "Oh, oh, oh, oh!" She walked around the house for, like, an hour, "Oh, oh, oh!" (Now Erica is doing a hysterical duck walk and groaning.)

'My dad called the middle wife. She delivers babies, but she doesn't have a sign on the car like the Domino's man. They got my mum to lie down in bed like this ...' (Erica lies down with her back against the wall.)

'And then, pop! My mum had this bag of water she kept in there in case he got thirsty, and it just blew up and spilled all over the bed, like psshhheew!' (Erica has her legs spread with her hands miming water flowing away.)

'Then the middle wife starts saying "push, push", and "breathe, breathe". They started counting, but never even got past ten. Then all of a sudden, out comes my brother. He was covered in yucky stuff that they all said was from mum's play-centre so there must be a lot of toys inside there. When he got out, the middle wife spanked him for crawling up in there.'

Erica stood up, took a big bow and returned to her seat.

What is the sun made of?

The sun is a big yellow circle made out of really soft, hot material.
Alyssa, 4

Hot gas, because my dad told me. The flames make it hot, and the flames come from the matches down here on earth.
Michael, 4

White and blue, 'cause I can see sky when I look at the sun.
Jett, 4

The sun is made of sunshine.
Harry, 4

It is made of yellow.
Kaia, 4

It is made of hot because you can feel it hot on your head.
Oscar, 4

It is made of a flower, 'cause it is yellow.
Rohan, 4

Where does the moon go at night?

Up into the sky.
Michael, 4

It goes down under the floor, under every floor.
Fred, 3

Where did all the dinosaurs go?

I think they went into the earth. They died because they
ate too much food, maybe not healthy food, so they died.
Alyssa, 4

I don't know, I think back to the dinosaur shop.
Max, 4

In a cave. All in together, and they played.
Freddie, 3

They went in the water to swim.
Jett, 4

They died, because they were stinked.
Sharks lived before dinosaurs but sharks are still alive.
Rory, 4

They went into kindy.
Kaia, 4

Um ... into dinosaur world.
Harry, 4

Love and romance

When you love somebody, your eyelashes go up and down
and little stars come out of you.
Karen, 7

Love is when a girl puts on perfume and a boy puts on shaving
cologne and they go out and smell each other.
Karl, 5

Love is like a butterfly kissing your cheek, sometimes like
my heart will burst.
Siobhan, 9

Your heart pumps, you get butterflies (with a crush). With
friends you just feel joyful at seeing them and with parents
you cry at thinking about your parents leaving you (death).
Isabel, 13

You might go on a date or say do you want to come with me ...
but it's pretty disgusting for kids.
Holly, 8

Intimate moments

(While helping hang socks on the clothesline)
Mummy, you can have socks with daddy if you like.
Ava, 3

Adella, 3: Mummy ... I have something to tell you ...
Mummy: What is it, darling?
Adella: I'm pregnant ... and I don't know what to do
(cue make-believe tears).

*(After overhearing her mother and aunt discussing
the end of her aunt's relationship)*
We need to call him straight away and tell him that's
a putdown and it's not okay.
Ava M, 5

All about mummy

(Introducing her mother)
This is my daughter, mummy.
Stella V, 3

(Pointing to a tattoo on mummy's back)
Who did that drawing on you, mummy?
Jasper, 2

Mummy, when I have my kids you will be dead old.
Lucy, 4

Mum, that dress is so pretty I could cry ...
I've never seen you look so delightful.
Ava, 5

*(While watching her non-cooking mother cleaning
up the kitchen one night)*
Mum, did you know that in the olden days the
mummies did the cooking?
Sophie, 9

You're ruining my life, mummy! I'm telling my fairy godmother.
Olivia, 2

C'mon mum, put some back into it.
Benjamin, 3

Mother love

Mum, I'll still love you even when you are very old.
Georgia, 4

I love my mummy 'cause she gives us chocolate in the shower.
Jett, 4

My mummy loves me more than anybody. You don't see anyone else
kissing me to sleep at night.
Clare, 6

How to make my mum happy

By being nice to your sister and not bickering with them.
Also going shopping with her even though it's really boring.
Charlotte, 11

By saying 'I love you' and giving her handmade things.
Mackenzie, 10

Give her a hug, a squeezy hug, and hold her hand lots.
Siobhan, 9

By liking her.
Sienna, 6

What makes my mum cross

Doing a fluff in her face.
Aidan, 5

Doing karate kicks on her.
Lincoln, 5

When we leave the back door open and the chickens
come in and poo on the carpet.
Charlotte, 11

Waking her up in the middle of the night. Then she's really mad –
that's why I prefer to wake up my dad.
Isabel, 13

All about daddy

Dad, you got big boobs like mum.
Jacob, 3

Daddy, when you die can I have your car?
Rosa, 4

(After dad tied her shoelaces)
You did it, dad. You are a rock star!
Georgia, 4

When your dad is mad and asks you 'Do I look stupid?', don't answer.
Heather, 16

Don't pull dad's finger when he tells you to.
Emily, 10

During my piano recital, I was on a stage and I was scared.
I looked at all the people watching me, and saw my daddy waving
and smiling. He was the only one doing that. I wasn't scared anymore.
Cindy, 8

How to make my dad happy

Playing on the Wii with him and jumping on the trampoline.
Siena, 8

Make him a surprise like a special tie.
Niamh, 5

Pull a funny face.
Eve, 5

My dad is always happy when I do well at being his little
girl and being myself.
Shona, 12

Buy him chocolate and a new bike (the new bike has
to be better than his old one).
Helena, 13

What makes my dad cross

If I smack his bum.
Eve, 5

Mummy loves daddy

Love is when my mummy makes coffee for my daddy and she
takes a sip before giving it to him, to make sure the taste is okay.
Danny, 7

Love is when mummy gives daddy the best piece of chicken.
Elaine, 5

Love is when mummy sees daddy on the toilet and she
doesn't think it's gross.
Mark, 6

Love is when mummy sees daddy smelly and sweaty and
still says he is handsomer than Robert Redford.
Chris, 7

Love is when you kiss all the time. Then when you get tired
of kissing, you still want to be together and you talk more.
My mummy and daddy are like that. They look gross when they kiss.
Emily, 8

Why God made mums

Answers given by second-grade school children to the following questions.

Why did God make mothers?
· She's the only one who knows where the sticky tape is.
· Mostly to clean the house.
· To help us out of there when we were getting born.

How did God make mothers?
· He used dirt, just like for the rest of us.
· Magic plus super powers and a lot of stirring.
· God made my mum just the same like he made me. He just used bigger parts.

What ingredients are mothers made of?
· God makes mothers out of clouds and angel hair and everything nice in the world and one dab of mean.
· They had to get their start from men's bones. Then they mostly use string, I think.

Why did God give you your mother and not some other mum?
· We're related.
· God knew she likes me a lot more than other people's mums like me.

What kind of little girl was your mum?
· My mum has always been my mum and none of that other stuff.
· I don't know because I wasn't there, but my guess would be pretty bossy.
· They say she used to be nice.

What did your mum need to know about your dad before she married him?
· His last name.
· She had to know his background. Like is he a crook? Does he get drunk on beer?
· Does he make at least $800 a year? Did he say NO to drugs and YES to chores?

Why did your mum marry your dad?
· My dad makes the best spaghetti in the world. And my mum eats a lot.
· She got too old to do anything else with him.
· My grandma says that mum didn't have her thinking cap on.

Who's the boss at your house?
· Mum doesn't want to be boss, but she has to because dad's such an idiot.
· Mum. You can tell by room inspection. She sees the stuff under the bed.
· I guess mum is, but only because she has a lot more to do than dad.

What's the difference between mums and dads?
- Mums work at work and work at home and dads just go to work at work.
- Mums know how to talk to teachers without scaring them.
- Dads are taller and stronger, but mums have all the real power 'cause that's who you got to ask if you want to sleep over at your friend's.
- Mums have magic, they make you feel better without medicine.

What does your mum do in her spare time?
- Mothers don't have spare time.
- To hear her talk, she pays bills all day long.

What would it take to make your mum perfect?
- On the inside she's already perfect. Outside, I think some kind of plastic surgery.
- You know, her hair. I'd dye it, maybe blue.

If you could change one thing about your mum, what would it be?
- She has this weird thing about me keeping my room clean. I'd get rid of that.
- I'd make my mum smarter. Then she would know it was my sister who did it and not me.
- I would like her to get rid of those invisible eyes on the back of her head.

This is love

Love is when people hug each other and kiss each other
and they don't punch or hit.
Kimmi, 5

Love is when you go out to eat and give somebody most of your
French fries without making them give you any of theirs.
Chrissy, 6

Love is when you tell a guy you like his shirt, then he wears it every day.
Noelle, 7

Love is like a little old woman and a little old man who are
still friends even after they know each other so well.
Tommy, 6

Love is what makes you smile when you're tired.
Terri, 4

When my grandmother got arthritis, she couldn't bend over and paint her toenails anymore. So my grandfather does it for her all the time, even when his hands got arthritis too. That's love.
Rebecca, 8

If you want to learn to love better, you should start with a friend who you hate.
Nikka, 6

When someone loves you, the way they say your name is different. You just know that your name is safe in their mouth.
Billy, 4

Love is what's in the room with you at Christmas if you stop opening presents and listen.
Bobby, 7

You really shouldn't say 'I love you' unless you mean it. But if you mean it, you should say it a lot. People forget.
Jessica, 8

My family

A family is where you care for others like your mum and dad,
your baby and cousins and stuff.
Mia, 7

A group of people connected together by love and they
also can be related.
Isabelle, 12

A group of people with the same last name.
Mackenzie B, 10

(Naquahn, 4, has dark skin. Mum and his little sister are fair skinned.)
I am brown because I drink lots of chocolate milk.
They are white because they only drink white milk.

Rules for family life

Don't pick on your sister when she's holding a baseball bat.
Joel, 10

When you get a bad grade in school, show it to your mum
when she's on the phone.
Alyesha, 13

Never allow your three-year-old brother in the same room
as your school assignment.
Traci, 14

When you want something expensive, ask your grandparents.
Matthew, 12

Remember you're never too old to hold your father's hand.
Molly, 11

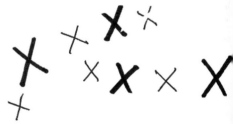

Discipline

Dad: I am very sad because you didn't clean up your mess.
Alexander, 4: Just look at the stars, dad, and that will make you feel better.

(On being sent to her room for talking back)
Daddy was a bit harsh – I was only telling him that 'shut up' was rude.
Stella R, 8

You can be dad, I will be mum – 'cause she makes the rules.
Jack H, 3

How could you smack me, mummy? You're my princess!
Jack W, 3

(Explaining to her mum that it wasn't her being naughty, but her soft toy 'baby jaguar'.)
Mum: If baby jaguar continues to do naughty things then he will have to sit in the laundry and you won't be allowed to visit him.
Charli, 4: Baby jaguar has told me that I should call you a 'bitch'.

What mummy and daddy do all day

Look after the house, feed your pet, go to work to learn
some things they haven't already learnt at school.
Holly I, 8

They both 'work'. Mum is at home, cleaning and caring for my sister.
My dad is at work, having coffee and socialising at lunch.
Isabel, 13

My dad goes to work counting things and my mum cleans the
house and does the shopping.
Georgia, 9

They go to work, collect money, take their daughter to ballet.
Aidan, 5

Dad would get to work at 4am then work till 9pm with
non-stopping paperwork.
Mackenzie, 10

Their days are boring – but actually I think mum and dad
think they have fun days.
Siobhan, 9

Being a grown-up: the best bits

Looking after your own darlings.
Majella, 8

You can drive a car and you know where you're driving and you know how much money to spend and you can buy a house and all sorts of other things.
Aidan, 5

The best thing is you get to stay up late.
Tara, 7

You can eat chocolate.
Clancy, 6

You can make all the rules.
Kimmi, 5

You can have babies.
Sienna, 6

I could get more jewellery and high heels.
Evie, 5

Being a grown-up: the worst bits

You don't get to run around because you're big.
Holly, 8

You have to do boring stuff.
Clancy, 6

You can't do as many things that you could do as a kid.
Aidan, 5

Maybe it's hard finding a husband or wife.
Gracie, 7

Sometimes you have to shout over voices.
Kimmi, 5

You have to do all the jobs.
Sienna, 6

The worst thing is you have to make dinner.
Tara, 7

When I grow up, I want to be ...

A Jedi. Learn kung fu. Be a scientist and an artist.
Aidan, 5

An artist. You can paint things and it's good to have
an activity to do during the day.
Holly, 8

An architect because it would earn me lots of money
and get me through life with no problems.
Mackenzie B, 10

A policeman – so I can arrest our school.
Lincoln, 5

I was born to be a hero.
Finn, 2

Getting older

Mum, I don't want to get old ... I want to stay new.
Karl, 4

When I grow up I don't want to be an adult anyway.
I want to be a fireman.
Harry P, 4

Pa, I wish you were younger. We could play together all the time.
Austin, 9

Mummy, daddy, if you are not dead when I get married, I will
invite you to my wedding.
Stella V, 7

Adults don't know how to play; they only know how to work.
Jack, 4

It's not that great being an adult. It just means you're closer to dying.
Oscar, 5

Why do people die?

So God can have some company.
Mia, 7

People die because they were made with a beginning and an end.
Shona, 12

People die because they don't eat much food.
Evie, 5

Either they think there's no point in living or they have lived their life.
Yadanar, 12

Well, everyone has to die or the earth will be crowded and we won't have anywhere to live. Some people might have to live in the ocean.
Charlotte, 11

Because that's what life is about.
Niamh, 5

Where do people go when they die?

A cemetery. Their shadow goes up to heaven.
Mia, 7

On the ground. They get buried and turn into ghosts.
Charlie S, 5

Mum: Oliver, we're going to take some flowers for our friend
as her mum was very sick and died.
Oliver, 3: Are we going to send the flowers to heaven?

Mum: Oliver, Grampa died last night but he is in heaven now and will
always watch over us.
Oliver (pointing up to the ceiling): Look up there, mum, it's Grampa's eye!

What is heaven like?

Heaven is very white and has people floating in it and
God sitting up in a chair.
Georgia, 9

Cloudy and full of angels. Jesus lives there.
Stafford, 8

A calm white fluffy clouded place with no deaths or fights.
Mackenzie, 10

Underground but nice. Where everyone is happy and safe.
Sienna, 6

Everyone loves everyone else. You get to see Jesus every day.
You see dead people who believe in Jesus.
Isabel, 13

When I go to heaven, I want to ride a gryphon and see the
nest of a phoenix.
Alexa, 6

Heaven is like a graveyard.
Lincoln, 5

What is God like?

He's someone who was in our world a long, long time ago. He was the only one around. She takes care of everyone and she makes you.
Aidan, 5

A mountain. He makes the weather.
Charlie, 5

He has a girlfriend and a baby. He helps you.
Eve S, 5

He cares for you and he protects you. God is a very nice person who has a tiny bit of blood on him and a white dress and grey hair.
Georgia, 9

A boy and a girl mixed together who made the world.
Majella, 8

Isis. It just sits in the sky and watches over people. If they need help the god will help them instead.
Kimmi, 5

Some of the kids at school say that God is everywhere but if that's true, he's in our chairs and we are sitting on him.
Alexa, 6

Messages for God

Get rid of all the bad people. Stop transport polluting,
make cars differently.
Siobhan, 9

Stop war and also financial crises. The parliament is very
worried about it.
Charlotte, 11

Don't change anything – the world is a good place as it is
and by changing things it may wreck it. Anything that needs
to happen can happen naturally.
Sophia, 10

Messages from God

This morning before I woke up, God told me I am
beautiful like a butterfly.
Finn, 4

Today at preschool when I was sleeping God told me I would die
when I am 120. He told me lots of other stuff before I was born.
But I don't remember any of that now. I will remember it again
when I go to heaven.
Finn B, 4

Acknowledgements

My deepest thanks to the following people:

Everyone who contributed quotes and sayings to this book: Jenny Amosa, Rebecca Austin, Nicola Baartse, Helen Bain, Kay Benson, Victoria Bladen, Sandy Brauer, Angela Briton, Helen Brodie, Lindar Butler, Michaela Butterworth, Michelle Carr-Brown, Karen Castle, Maree Clancy, Ian Collings, Joanne Cordery, Michele Corin, Vicki Creagan, Colin Dayman, Janis Fischer, Jane Frosh, Amey Garwood, Michelle Gibson, Rebecca Glasgow, Anna & Cameron Goffage, Daniel Graham, Angela Hardie, Ross & Lisa Harper, Gavin Hassan, Nicolle Heikkinen, Karen & Mitch Holmes, Alison Horsburgh, Jennifer Houston, Annie Hughes, Jessica Jackson, Lindsay Kasprowicz, Sharon Keeler, Sandra Kent, Marijke van Klinken, Belinda Longley, Meg MacLeod, Kay Marco, Jenny McGrath, Jan-Maree McGregor, Sandra Mulqueeney, Diana Nielson, Patricia Noble, Cath Nunnink, Liz Parr, Elissa Phillips, Maggie Ritchie, Kathryn Roulstone, Louise Sawyer, Nadine Shaw, Vicki Shepherd, Paul Sinnige, Renay Stevens, Katie Thirkhill, Annalisa Toole, Rod & Linda Trevor, Angelina Tut, Briony Tyquin, Wendy Walker, Toni Ward, Jessica White, Sarah Willmott, Michelle Wirkus, Melanie Wright, Katiemay.

My expert panel of teachers, child carers, curriculum experts and wise mothers, who vetted material for me: Virginia Beaufort, Anne Grant, Helen Jeremy, Wendy Walker and Libby Wark.

The schools, kindergartens and teachers who participated in group discussions and questionnaires as part of the gathering process for this book: children and students at C&K Paddington Community Kindergarten (teachers Belinda Ross and Vicki Hall), Rainworth State School (principal Bill Carey) and St Aidan's Anglican Girls School (principal Karen Spiller and Head of Library Services Kristen Lewis).

And as always, an enormous thanks goes to my family, both close (Robert, Bethany and Sophia) and further afield. Your support makes it possible.